Alexander Twilight

Alexander Twilight
(Courtesy of the Orleans County Historical Society)

Alexander Twilight

Vermont's African-American Pioneer

Michael T. Hahn

The New England Press, Inc.
Shelburne, Vermont

Manufactured in the United States of America
First Edition
Cover illustration by Alan Nahigian

For additional copies of this book or for a catalog of our other titles, please write:

The New England Press
P.O. Box 575
Shelburne, VT 05482

or e-mail: nep@together.net

Visit us on the Web at www.nepress.com

Hahn, Michael T., 1953-
    Alexander Twilight: Vermont's African-American pioneer / Michael
T. Hahn. -- 1st ed.
        p. cm.
    Includes bibliographic references and index.
    Summary: A biography of the noted educator who was the first
African American to graduate from an American college and the first
to serve on a state legislature.
    ISBN 1-881535-31-2
    1. Twilight, Alexander Lucius, 1795-1857--Juvenile literature.
2. Afro-American pioneers--Vermont--Biography--Juvenile literature.
3. Pioneers--Vermont--Biography--Juvenile literature. 4. Afro-
American legislators--Vermont--Biography--Juvenile literature.
5. Educators--Vermont--Biography--Juvenile literature. 6. Vermont--
Biography--Juvenile literature. [1. Twilight, Alexander Lucius,
1795-1857. 2. Legislators. 3. Educators. 4. Afro-Americans--
Biography.] I. Title.
F53.T95H34   1998
974.3'00496073'0092--dc21
    [B]   98-31224
                                                              CIP
                                                              AC

CONTENTS

FOREWORD

The charismatic headmaster of Brownington Academy in the rugged hills of northern Vermont not far south of the Canadian border, Alexander Twilight was a compelling man: a teacher, preacher, legislator, and, most important, the first African-American to graduate from an American college (Middlebury College, 1823).

As Michael Hahn's fine new biography of Twilight makes clear, he was also a complex figure, flourishing in the frontier openness of nineteenth-century Vermont, which afforded him the elbow room he needed to pursue his unique vision. Not only did Twilight build his own school, stone by stone, but he taught it in his own way, combining rigorous scholarship with a great sense of fun that his nearly 3,000 students remembered with delight all their lives.

In *Alexander Twilight: Vermont's African-American Pioneer*, Hahn, the author of acclaimed biographies of the famed

Revolutionary War figures Ethan Allen and Ann Story and a native Vermonter himself, has combined painstaking research with engaging storytelling to bring this important American educator and African-American to life in a way that will appeal to readers of all ages, in Vermont and beyond.

Howard Frank Mosher
Irasburg, Vermont

ACKNOWLEDGMENTS

I would like to extend my sincere thanks to Tracy Martin, Howard Frank Mosher, Bob Buckeye, John M. Lovejoy, Robert Michaud, Mark Wanner, and especially my dedicated wife, Robin Tarwater Hahn, for helping to make this book a reality.

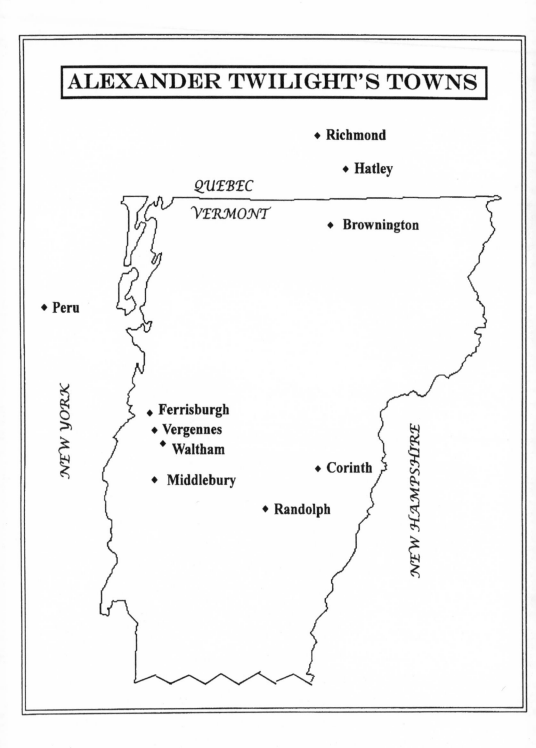

ALEXANDER TWILIGHT'S TOWNS

• Richmond

• Hatley

QUEBEC

VERMONT

• Brownington

• Peru

NEW YORK

• Ferrisburgh

• Vergennes

• Waltham

• Corinth

• Middlebury

NEW HAMPSHIRE

• Randolph

INTRODUCTION

Alexander Twilight was, first and foremost, a man of great vision and determination who worked hard his entire life. Famous in his day as a teacher, builder, and legislator, he is best known now as the first African-American to graduate from an American college and the first to serve in a state legislature. His greatest achievements had nothing to do with his race, however. Instead, they demonstrate how someone with intelligence and ambition can overcome almost any obstacle.

Today, Alexander's most obvious legacy is the Old Stone House, a massive structure he built in Brownington, Vermont. According to legend, Alexander constructed the huge granite building by himself, helped only by an ox. The building now serves as a museum operated by the Orleans County Historical Society.

Alexander's effect on people was less visible, but it was likely more important than his durable building. In

1

fact, during twenty-seven years of teaching, Alexander educated nearly 3,000 students and helped shape a generation of Northeast Kingdom residents.

Alexander Twilight overcame a humble childhood to become a scholar, a licensed preacher, a good husband, a legislator, a famous instructor, and the builder of an astonishing granite structure that still serves to educate people.

ALEXANDER'S YOUTH

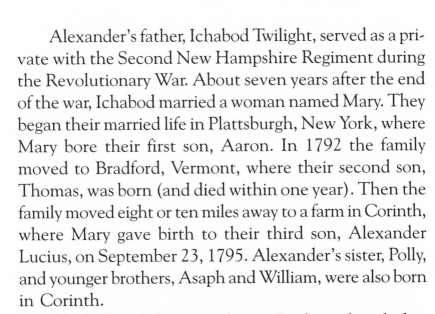

Alexander's father, Ichabod Twilight, served as a private with the Second New Hampshire Regiment during the Revolutionary War. About seven years after the end of the war, Ichabod married a woman named Mary. They began their married life in Plattsburgh, New York, where Mary bore their first son, Aaron. In 1792 the family moved to Bradford, Vermont, where their second son, Thomas, was born (and died within one year). Then the family moved eight or ten miles away to a farm in Corinth, where Mary gave birth to their third son, Alexander Lucius, on September 23, 1795. Alexander's sister, Polly, and younger brothers, Asaph and William, were also born in Corinth.

Ichabod Twilight was a farmer. In those days, before the invention of tractors and other farm machinery, farmers relied on livestock and their own muscles to do the heavy work needed to run a farm. Like most farm children of that era, Alexander learned how to work soon after he learned how to walk.

Life for most Vermont farm families at that time was hard and simple. They owned few store-bought possessions, and they spent most of their time working. During their rare moments of free time, they had to amuse themselves, because there was little entertainment available. But they enjoyed rural pastimes such as hunting, fishing, swimming in the summer, and sledding in the winter. Although they did not have fancy toys or other things that were not necessary for survival, they were usually able to raise enough food to keep from going hungry, and crime was rare. Families and communities supported each other during hard times, but most of the time they took care of themselves.

Ichabod Twilight was a mulatto, meaning that he had mixed black and white ancestry. Historians disagree about whether Mary, Alexander's mother, was black or white, but the Corinth town records describe Mary and Ichabod as "both colored." In the male-dominated society of that time, wives were often regarded as dependent upon their husbands, so Mary might have been listed as black simply because she had married an African-American. Whatever Mary's race, it is clear that her children were quite light-skinned for African-Americans.

Because of the color of their skin, life was even more difficult for the Twilight family than for other Vermont farm families. While the Twilights were scratching out a living in Corinth, most African-Americans worked as slaves on plantations. A slave was a person who was owned by another person and had no rights or freedom. The owner was legally allowed to force a slave to do anything.

Families were often split apart when slave children, destined never to see their parents again, were sold to different masters. Black slaves in the southern United States were forbidden by law to own property or get an education. Even their lives were not their own—an owner could legally kill a slave if he chose to do so.

Trading slaves to the British colonies was outlawed in 1807, when Alexander Twilight was twelve years old, but owning slaves was still legal. And shipping slaves continued illegally. In 1850 about 50,000 slaves per year were still being smuggled into America. It wasn't until 1865, when Alexander had been dead for eight years, that the Thirteenth Amendment to the United States Constitution ended slavery in the United States.

There was no slavery in Vermont when Alexander was a boy, but there was no doubt plenty of prejudice. The Twilights probably faced unfair behavior by people who didn't know that everyone should be judged on their merit rather than their race or color.

There is no denying that Ichabod was a man of color. *The History of Corinth, Vermont*, calls Ichabod "the first negro to settle in Corinth." In the United States at that time, any person with a bit of African blood was regarded as a negro. Some historians believe that Ichabod's mixed race was the basis for his last name, Twilight, which describes the half-light between sunset and darkness.

Years later the Census of 1840 listed Alexander and his brother Aaron with the group "Free White Persons." Aaron's death certificate describes him as white. Alexander's death certificate does not list his race. Asaph Twilight, one of Alexander's younger brothers, is called white on his marriage certificate. The only known photograph of Alexander, taken when he was middle-aged, doesn't clearly show his skin color. People who knew him as an adult sometimes described Alexander as "swarthy" or "bronzed."

Despite their father's racial mix, Alexander and his siblings were apparently able to pass for white. There is no record of Alexander ever mentioning his racial background. At a time when African-Americans suffered cruel prejudice, it is possible that as an adult Alexander intentionally chose to ignore his heritage. Perhaps the issue never came up because it simply seemed irrelevant to him. But when Alexander was a young boy living with his dark-skinned father, his racial background was obvious.

According to the Federal census, 557 African-Americans lived in Vermont in 1800. Vermont might not have been a paradise for them, but the Green Mountain State was probably one of the best places in the United States for blacks to live. Slavery had never been allowed in Vermont, and black people had the right to own land. In 1798, when Alexander was three years old, Ichabod Twilight took advantage of that right and bought a farm in Corinth.

The difference between owning land and working someone else's land as a tenant farmer was important. Tenant farmers could never get ahead because part of their profits always went to the landowner. Buying enough land to raise plenty of crops and livestock was the best way for poor families to improve their financial situation and work their way into the middle class. When Ichabod Twilight bought his farm in Corinth, he purchased a piece of the American Dream.

Unfortunately for the Twilight family, though, money was still a problem. They struggled to scrape together enough money to buy the farm, and as the years passed and they had more children, their finances declined. After five years Ichabod decided that he would have to seek work away from home. In 1803 Ichabod deeded the property to his oldest son, Aaron, despite the fact that Aaron was only twelve years old.

Ichabod departed to look for work and left Mary with five children struggling to run a hill farm. As it became harder and harder to keep her family fed, Mary faced some difficult choices. Finally she decided to indenture Alexander to a neighboring farmer until he was twenty-one years old.

Indentured servants surrendered their freedom to work for a master for a specific length of time. Some people volunteered to become indentured for financial reasons. For example, a poor person in Europe might have agreed to become an indentured servant for several years in exchange for the cost of a voyage to America. Other people were forced to become indentured because they had failed to pay their debts, or because they were criminals who were put to work instead of serving time in jail. Alexander's mother volunteered to have her son indentured for financial reasons, and she hoped that his indentureship would be similar to an apprenticeship and teach him the trade of farming.

Alexander Twilight was eight years old when he was indentured to a farmer named William Bowen, who owned the property bordering the Twilight farm. Although Alexander was able to sleep at home, he walked to and from the Bowen farm daily, and he spent little time with his family. Being forced into hard labor at such a young age must have been a painful experience. For the next twelve years Alexander worked hard on the

Bowen farm. He also learned how to read, which enabled him to leave his life as a farmer when his time on the Bowen farm ended.

Many people believe that Alexander was somehow able to save up a little money over the years, because when he was twenty years old, he was able to buy back the final year of his indentureship. There is no proof of this. The Bowens may have simply discharged him sooner than usual, or maybe someone else paid for it. Regardless of how he was able to get it, Alexander used his extra year to get started right away on his formal education.

In 1815 Alexander enrolled in the Orange County Grammar School in Randolph, a town twenty miles southwest of Corinth. In those days a grammar school was a place where students prepared for college. Alexander studied at Randolph for six years, completing the secondary-school courses plus two college-level courses, and graduated in 1821.

While he was in school, Alexander worked hard to support himself and his studies. Driven by a strong ambition, Alexander was determined not to let his challenging childhood hold him back. He thought that if he believed in himself and always tried to do his best, there was no limit to what he could achieve.

Alexander lived in a time and place when people could move up in the world through self-discipline and hard work. New Englanders became famous for their work ethic as they strived to improve life for themselves and their children. Alexander learned this lesson at an early age, and his willingness to work hard under difficult conditions enabled him to accomplish amazing things.

MIDDLEBURY COLLEGE

In 1821, when Alexander Twilight was twenty-six years old, he enrolled at Middlebury College. Because he had completed college courses at Randolph, Alexander entered Middlebury as a third-year student. It had taken him a long time to reach college, but the important thing was that he had finally reached his goal. Alexander knew that a good education was the key to success.

Located in the Champlain Valley of western Vermont, Middlebury College was founded in 1800 to educate students in the tradition of the liberal arts. Middlebury's faculty and student body remain devoted to learning to this day, and the college is among the most prestigious liberal arts colleges in the country.

At Middlebury Alexander studied surveying, trigonometry, philosophy, navigation, astronomy, theology, composition, logic, Greek, German, Hebrew, chemistry, mineralogy, and other subjects. He paid $32.00 per year

9

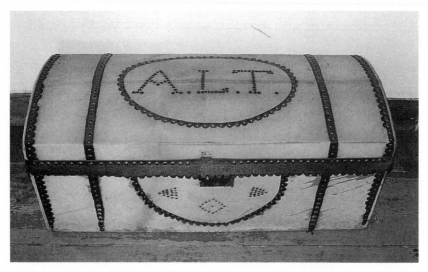
Tacks arranged in the shape of his initials decorate Alexander's trunk. (Author photo)

for tuition and expenses, plus an additional $58.50 per year for his meals.

Alexander graduated from Middlebury College in August 1823 and became the first African-American to earn a college degree in America. Two other colleges, Amherst and Bowdoin, graduated black men three years later.

Nowadays Middlebury College is justly proud of the fact that they were the first American college to graduate an African-American. Middlebury has an honorable history of being among the first colleges to admit racial minorities, women, Jews, and others who faced discrimination. The African-American Alliance is a prominent student organization on campus, and about 20 percent of Middlebury's undergraduates are students of color. Seeking diversity, the college developed the Twilight Program (named after Alexander) to invite minority teachers, scholars, and artists to Middlebury College.

When Alexander Twilight applied to Middlebury, however, the college was probably unaware of his racial background. In the 1830s, more than a decade after Alexander graduated from college, a black man named Andrew Harris applied to Middlebury College and was denied acceptance because, he was informed, Middlebury College had a policy against accepting negroes. Harris was later accepted at the University of Vermont, where he graduated in 1838.

The second African-American to attend Middlebury College was Martin Freeman, who was accepted in 1845 and graduated in 1849. The fact that twenty-two years passed between Alexander's graduation and Freeman's acceptance seems to indicate that Middlebury College, like many schools at that time, was reluctant to admit African-Americans.

Years later Middlebury College Dean Walter E. Howard, who graduated from Middlebury in 1871, was quoted as saying that Twilight was a negro, so obviously the faculty at Middlebury became aware of Alexander's race at some point. It is doubtful that the faculty was aware of his race when he applied, however, or they probably would have responded to Alexander's application in the same way that they responded to the application of Andrew Harris. On the other hand, it is possible that the policy not to admit came after Alexander attended Middlebury. There is no record of when the policy began or when it ended.

The milestone in African-American history doubtless meant little or nothing to Alexander at the time. He cared only that he had gotten his college degree, and he was eager to begin the next phase of his life.

STARTING A LIFETIME

Committed to putting his education to good use, Alexander accepted a job teaching school in Peru, New York, a remote town in the Adirondack Mountains. Alexander discovered that he enjoyed teaching, and his love for the job made him a very good teacher. He soon realized, though, that he wanted to serve the community in another way too—he wanted to become a preacher. One of the subjects Alexander had studied at Middlebury College was theology, which is the theory of religious ideas and beliefs.

Alexander also found time for romance. He met a white woman in Peru named Mercy Ladd Merrill, and they fell in love. Mercy was the daughter of Dudley and Polly Merrill, a respected and prosperous couple from Unity, New Hampshire. When they married in 1826, Mercy was twenty-one years old and Alexander was thirty-one. Since Alexander had so much energy and drive, the

Mercy Twilight. (Courtesy of the Orleans County Historical Society)

difference in their ages was probably not a problem. There is no evidence that the difference in their racial backgrounds was ever an issue either.

Alexander pursued his desire to become a preacher, and in 1827 the Champlain Presbytery in Plattsburgh issued him a license to preach. The Presbyterians were opening frontier missions throughout New England. Individual Presbyterian congregations elect their own elders, including the minister, who together govern the church. The minister usually serves as moderator and is ordained and disciplined by the next level of church organization, which traditionally consists of equal numbers of ordained ministers and lay elders.

Presbyterian worship is simple and orderly. It revolves around preaching from the Scriptures and singing hymns based on the Psalms in the Bible. Two sacraments are recognized: the Lord's Supper, which is usually celebrated monthly or quarterly, and baptism, which is administered to the infant children of church members.

When he was ordained, Alexander was in his fourth year of teaching in Peru. Soon afterwards he took advantage of an opportunity to put his preaching skills to work while remaining a teacher. He took a job teaching in Vergennes, Vermont, and every weekend he walked to the neighboring towns of Waltham and Ferrisburgh to preach. The people in Waltham and Ferrisburgh wanted a minister, but neither town was able to hire a full-time preacher, so Alexander preached in Waltham on one Sunday and in Ferrisburgh the next.

It was a three-mile walk to Ferrisburgh and more than four miles to Waltham, so Alexander needed to walk six to nine miles round-trip every Sunday through rain, hot summer sun, and winter snowstorms. Alexander brought the same focus and dedication to his new job that had made him a success as a teacher, scholar, and everything else he attempted. People took notice of Alexander's abilities, and after serving for a year in the Vergennes area, Alexander was offered a position in Brownington, Vermont, a thriving farming community near the Canadian border that was to become the scene of his greatest accomplishments.

BROWNINGTON

The town of Brownington is located about forty miles to the northeast of where it was originally situated. An area including the present town of Johnson was once known as Brownington, but ownership of the land was disputed.

In 1782 a pair of brothers from Connecticut named Timothy and Daniel Brown, along with sixty-four of their associates, were granted land east of Cambridge for their service in the Revolutionary War. A man named William Johnson held a claim to the same land, however, and Johnson and the Browns argued about the land for years. They appealed to the governor and the assembly, who then argued amongst themselves about how to resolve the problem. Finally the Browns agreed to settle for a grant of different land to the northeast, where Brownington is today.

The Republic of Vermont issued Brownington a charter in 1790. Nobody lived there at that time, and in order to formally organize as a town, twenty families needed to move in. Timothy and Daniel Brown never settled in Brownington themselves. Instead they sold their land to real estate speculators, who divided the land into separate lots and sold the lots to other settlers. Most of the settlers were of British ancestry, and they moved to Brownington from Connecticut, Massachusetts, Rhode Island, and southern New Hampshire.

During the years of 1791 to 1793, an explorer and trailblazer named Timothy Hinman built the Hinman Road from Greensboro to Derby. The Hinman Road passed through the primitive frontier towns of Glover, Barton, and Brownington. Considering the rough terrain and crude tools available, building the road was a remarkable feat.

The Hinman Road made Brownington a more attractive place to live, and in 1796 Peter Clark from Lyndeboro, New Hampshire, became the first permanent settler of Brownington. Peter Clark was a potter who had learned the earthenware craft from his father. Peter moved to Brownington with his wife and built a homestead. According to Brownington historian Edith Herrick, Peter opened his own pottery (quite an optimistic venture considering that the Clarks were the first family in town) and ran it for more than seventeen years. Peter also served as the first deacon of a Congregational Church that formed in Brownington in 1809.

Three years after the Clarks arrived, Brownington had assembled the twenty families needed to formally organize as a town. Most Brownington residents were farmers raising crops such as wheat, oats, hemp, hops, and flax and livestock such as cows, pigs, sheep, and poultry.

Town officers were elected in 1799, and soon Brownington became so important that it was named a half-shire town. A shire town was the county seat, where county court was held. Brownington and Craftsbury became half-shire towns, which meant that court was held in Brownington for one session and in Craftsbury for the next. The cellar of a Brownington building near the courthouse served as the county jail. The county seat was moved to Irasburg in 1816 (and later to Newport), but Brownington continued to thrive.

As the population increased in the Brownington area, the Hinman Road was used as a section of the stagecoach route between Concord, New Hampshire, and Stanstead, Quebec. Difficult terrain and unstable weather made traveling by stagecoach an adventure, but it was the best form of inland transportation available at the time. The fact that Brownington was located on the main stagecoach route joining Boston and Montreal helped the area develop rapidly.

Many former stagecoach routes are still called post roads because, in addition to travelers and luggage, the coaches carried mail. During the 1800s a busy post office was located in Brownington, and between 1800 and 1820 settlers came from as far away as Newport to collect their mail in Brownington.

In 1806 a New Hampshire newspaper printed an advertisement for 8,000 acres in Brownington selling for three dollars an acre. According to the advertisement, Brownington was home to fifty families plus mills for grinding grain and sawing lumber. One of the speculators who was selling the land was William Baxter, a young lawyer who would leave his mark on the town.

William Baxter served as the Vermont State's Attorney from 1802 until 1814, and later he became an assistant judge. In 1820 Baxter introduced a bill in the state legislature to build a grammar school in Orleans County. Derby and Craftsbury were the two largest towns in the county, and Brownington was located on a good road between the two towns, so Brownington was chosen as the location for a secondary school to serve the entire county.

During a town meeting in 1821, town residents selected a vacant lot near the top of a broad hill on the west side of the main road as the school site. Baxter paid to have a two-story, wooden frame schoolhouse built, and he gave it to the town with the condition that the second story of the building be used for religious meetings until a church could be built. The Orleans County Grammar School opened in 1823 and offered courses in algebra, astronomy, chemistry, geology, philosophy, trigonometry, English, French, Greek, and Latin to students who were preparing for college. Pupils came from throughout Orleans County to study at the Orleans County Grammar School, and they boarded with Brownington residents.

The school was maintained with funds collected as state lands' rent in Orleans County. When the school was five years old, it was being run by a man named Isaac Parker. Then the Brownington trustees decided to hire a young man who was gaining a solid reputation as an educator and minister: Alexander Twilight.

PREACHING, TEACHING, AND SPECULATING

Alexander became the principal of the Orleans County Grammar School in 1829, when Brownington was a prospering hilltop village with 400 residents. Alexander and Mercy stayed with a family named Spencer for a while, then they reportedly moved into a three-room house within walking distance of the school. The house may have been too small for Alexander's ambitions, because he immediately started to build a larger home in front of it.

Alexander's grand plans were supported by mysterious amounts of money. Soon after he arrived in Brownington, he began to buy land, and he invested more money than a man who earned only fifty dollars per twelve-week teaching session should have been able to afford. Within a month after moving to Brownington,

Soon after moving to Brownington, Alexander built this large house. Several students boarded here before Alexander completed Athenian Hall. (Author photo)

Alexander bought a sixty-acre farm located a few hundred yards from the school. He paid a local farmer named Cyrus Eaton $650 for the farm, apparently in cash because there is no record of any mortgage, only a warranty deed.

During the next seventeen years, Alexander bought and sold land at least thirty times. Even including the small amount of money that he made by preaching, there is no way that Alexander could have earned the thousands of dollars exchanged in those land deals. He certainly didn't inherit any money. One possible explanation for this mysterious cash is that Mercy brought a substantial dowry to the marriage.

Until the passage of laws granting women equal property rights in the nineteenth century, the property that a bride brought with her to marriage was called her dowry.

A large dowry improved her appeal as a wife, strengthened in-law family ties, and gave the newlyweds a financial start. A woman's dowry and other possessions traditionally became the property of the man she married. In some parts of the world, dowries are an important part of marriages to this day, but in the United States a husband and wife are equal partners.

Mercy's family, the Merrills, were not rich, but they were certainly successful, and it is likely that Mercy brought a generous dowry to the marriage. A large dowry would explain where Alexander's money came from, but there is no proof of its existence. It remains another Twilight mystery.

When Alexander moved to Brownington, the local churchgoers were still worshiping in the assembly room on the second floor of the school building. These worshipers were Congregationalists, a form of Protestant church organization based on the right of self-government of each congregation.

Traditionally Congregationalists opposed Presbyterians, who managed churches through district assemblies instead of allowing self-government of each church. This conflict might have posed a problem for Alexander, a Presbyterian preacher with Congregationalist followers. Fortunately, common sense prevailed among the worshipers. Alexander was ordained as a Congregationalist minister soon after arriving in Brownington, and he began preaching every Sunday on the second floor of he school.

Being a good husband, speculating in land, and preaching on the weekends kept Alexander busy, but he concentrated most of his attention on the school.

Alexander wanted to transform the Orleans County Grammar School into the biggest and best school possible, so he sought more students by placing advertisements in Vermont and eastern Quebec newspapers. Gradually the enrollment at the school expanded.

Only those students who resided in Brownington lived at home; the rest of the students boarded with families in town. As the number of students increased, the available space for boarders filled up. Alexander and Mercy boarded three boys and two girls in their big, new house, but more space was needed.

Alexander went to the school's trustees and asked them to raise funds to build a large dormitory. As so often happens, some of the trustees did not agree that a new dormitory was necessary, so they did not want to ask taxpayers for the money to build it. Although Alexander debated the issue several times and presented a good argument for the new building, he could not persuade enough trustees to get funding for the project. Most educators would have either accepted the trustees' decision or continued to dispute the matter. But Alexander Twilight was determined to build the best school ever to exist in the area, so he simply decided to pursue it on his own.

ATHENIAN HALL

Convinced that his school needed more space to house students, Alexander decided to build a large dormitory himself. In 1834, when he had lived and taught in Brownington for five years, he marked a foundation plan on the land across the dirt road from his home and started to build a huge granite structure.

At the time Alexander began construction, the building lot was still owned by neighboring farmers. The land wasn't deeded to Alexander until the spring of 1836, when the building was almost complete. On May 14, 1836, for "the consideration of one dollar," Portus and Carlos Baxter sold the land to Alexander with the condition that if the building were to be used for any other purpose than a dormitory, or if Alexander failed to maintain a "good and substantial board fence" between the farm and the dormitory, the land would revert back to the Baxters.

How Alexander paid for the building is something of a mystery. Neither the state, the county, nor the town of Brownington contributed any money for it. Historians credit Alexander with constructing the building at his own expense, but how could he possibly have afforded such a grand project? One possibility is that Alexander asked for contributions from Orleans County residents. Certainly some of the funding originally came from Cyrus Eaton.

Cyrus Eaton, the man who had sold Alexander his sixty-acre farm, owned the land beside the dormitory plot. When Alexander started building the dormitory, Cyrus had just finished building a new house next door. Cyrus was Alexander's friend, and he probably loaned him money. An 1841 record shows that Alexander owed Cyrus $940, which seems like a large amount when you consider that men were willing to work hard all day for $1.50.

Many years later, one of Cyrus Eaton's sons wrote in a letter that his father had helped Alexander build the Old Stone House. Eaton's help was probably in the form of money, but he may have helped with the actual construction too. Local legend claims that Alexander erected the building entirely by himself, but several historians believe that he probably had some assistance.

The town of Brownington has always been committed to preserving its history, and unlike many other towns, no fire or other disaster has destroyed the old records that help make Brownington an important historic district today. The fact that there are almost no documents or records of the construction of Alexander Twilight's building might imply that the town custodians intentionally overlooked the startling monument arising in their village. The trustees didn't agree with Alexander's conviction that a huge dormitory was needed. Although they left him in charge of the school, they offered him no funds or support of any kind for building the dormitory. When Alexander began to build it anyway, it appears that they ignored the project and let him persevere alone.

Even before he started construction work, Alexander had been nearly as busy as a person can be. Teaching at the school, preaching to his congregation, speculating in real estate, and helping Mercy run their home (where they still boarded several students) demanded all of his time and energy. When he decided to build the dormitory, Alexander knew that he needed to give up something, so he resigned as minister of the church. He hated to abandon preaching, but it was necessary if the dormitory was to be built.

As Alexander searched for building materials, lumber was an affordable and readily available option. Alexander wanted to create an important, permanent structure, though, so he decided to build with stone. Alexander's selection of a more challenging (and more permanent) material was an indication of his character. He found a supply of durable but difficult-to-use stone close to his building site.

The nearby fields were dotted with huge granite boulders that had been left behind by retreating glaciers. Glacial boulders were so plentiful in Vermont that they made farming difficult. In the 1800s farmers simply plowed around the big granite boulders in their fields. The boulders were a curse, and farmers near Brownington were delighted to have Alexander haul the granite off their land.

There are several different kinds of stones in Athenian Hall, which indicates that the stones came from different sites. Some of the granite Alexander used may have been quarried, but rounded edges on a few stones indicate that at least some of the blocks were split from boulders. Oral history states that some of the stones came from boulders on the Wilfred Young property, about half a mile from the building.

Granite is hard and durable, and it is abundant in mountainous areas. As Alexander soon discovered, granite is also very heavy and difficult to cut or move. Alexander wanted to build with blocks of granite, so the first thing he had to do was figure out how to split the boulders into chunks small enough to handle.

Alexander used a hammer and star drill to bore rows of 2½-inch holes into the boulders. Historians disagree about how he then split the boulders apart. Some people believe that he drove dry wooden pegs into the holes, then soaked the pegs with water until they expanded enough to crack the stone. Other people think that Alexander hammered iron wedges into the holes to fracture the boulders. Maybe he tried both methods, but during cold weather, he probably just poured water into the holes. When water freezes into ice, it expands enough to crack stone, and freezing water is sometimes called "poor man's dynamite." No matter what method Alexander used, drilling and splitting the boulders into slabs was hard work.

Alexander used a hammer and chisel to chip the split-off slabs into building blocks. The finished stones are about twelve inches high and ten inches thick. Most of the stones range in length from two feet to six feet, except for the long stones around the doorways and windows, which are eight feet or longer. Some of the larger stones weigh more than 1,100 pounds.

Alexander used an ox to help him move the stones to his building site. The ox wore a yoke (a wooden frame around its neck like a collar) and probably pulled a sledge, which is a strong sled with low runners used to slide heavy loads over snow. When loading and unloading, Alexander used an iron pry bar as a lever to move the stones on wooden rollers. Alexander needed more than 1,500 stones, because the dormitory he planned was thirty-six feet by sixty-six feet and four stories high.

Splitting the boulders was hard work and moving the stones to the site was exhausting, but those tasks were probably easy compared to lifting the stones into place as the walls grew taller. Without any modern machinery such as a crane, Alexander somehow managed to hoist the stones into position. Exactly how he did it is uncertain. Many people in the Brownington area believe that he built a ramp of dirt next to the walls and dragged the stones up the ramp with his ox. The ramp could have been removed after the building was completed. But no record of such a ramp exists.

Some people believe that Alexander used a bull wheel to lift the stones. A bull wheel is part of a derrick, a hoisting device similar to a crane used in the construction industry to lift and lower heavy weights. According to popular legend, Alexander used his ox to turn a bull wheel, which powered a heavy cable to raise the stones to a temporary platform that Alexander built inside the rising walls. As the walls grew higher, the platform and the ox were moved upwards.

As the story goes, when the walls were finished, the ox was stranded forty-one feet above the ground. Alexander tried to lead the ox down a staircase to the ground, but the animal was terrified of descending, and no amount of coaxing could convince the ox to walk down. He couldn't leave the animal up there forever, so Alexander reluctantly decided to slaughter the ox on the platform. The ox was butchered high above the dormitory, then served as the main course of a feast to celebrate the completion of the tremendous building and the noble animal that gave its life for the construction.

The legend of the ox being butchered on the platform is generally acknowledged as true in the Northeast Kingdom and makes a good story. On the other hand, it

Alexander prepared and used more than 1,500 stones, some weighing more than half a ton, to build Athenian Hall. The huge dormitory was 66 feet by 36 feet and four stories high. (Author photo)

is hard to believe that a man capable of assembling such a tremendous building would not be able to figure out a way to get the ox down. Maybe the ox was injured and needed to be destroyed anyway. Perhaps Alexander tried to lower the ox on a sling, and the animal became injured in the attempt. Or maybe a bull wheel was never really used, and Alexander built earthen ramp instead. No one will ever know for sure.

However he did it, the fact remains that within two years, Alexander built an incredible structure, the first public building made of granite in Vermont. The four-story building is twenty-four feet tall at the side walls and forty-one feet high at the gable ends. The insides of the granite walls are lined with brick and faced with plaster over thin strips of wood, known as laths. The total width of each wall is about twenty inches, thick enough to help keep warmth in the building during the winter and keep it from getting too hot during the summer.

Instead of a central furnace, Alexander built a large fireplace in the kitchen and used a small brazier in each room on the first two floors. A brazier was a metal container used to burn charcoal or hold hot coals from the kitchen fireplace. Each brazier was connected by a brick flue to a small chimney. Smoke and fumes from the braziers traveled through the flues and rose from the row of chimneys that lined each side of the roof. Later, iron stoves were added in a number of rooms.

Among the most expensive parts of the building were the sixty-five glass windows that Alexander put in. The windows were a necessary expense because the students needed plenty of light for reading and writing.

Although the toilet was invented sixty-one years before Alexander finished his building, few if any houses in northern New England had indoor plumbing, so Alexander built outhouses. Then he installed a clever system that supplied the kitchen with water by using rainwater. Every time it rained, water ran off the wooden-shingle roof into gutters along the eaves that funneled the water to a stone water tank at the back of the dormitory. A pipe laid under the kitchen floor carried water, pulled by gravity, from the tank to the kitchen.

Alexander built the dormitory as a place where his students could sleep, eat, and do their homework while continuing to attend classes in the wooden schoolhouse up the hill. Some classes may have been held in the stone building also, but the original wooden schoolhouse continued as the main classroom throughout the school's existence.

Bread was baked in the kitchen, and all of the meals for the school were prepared there. In addition to the kitchen, the first floor held five smaller rooms used as common space. The second and third floors were walled off into twenty smaller rooms, where boarding students slept. The fourth floor held a parlor and a twenty-by-forty-foot assembly room big enough for the entire school to gather together.

The granite dormitory was one of the biggest, strongest, and most impressive buildings in Vermont. Alexander wanted to give the building a name that was as grand as the structure. At that time, many people in Europe and America were interested in a revival of Greek culture and architecture. Even the United States Capitol had been influenced by the Greek Revival.

Alexander appreciated the Greek Revival form and the ideal of democracy associated with it, so he decided to name his building Athenian Hall. Athens is the capitol

The Orleans County Historical Society maintains Athenian Hall as a museum open to the public. (Author photo)

and largest city in Greece, and centuries ago Athens was the artistic and cultural center of the world.

Alexander's magnificent building might have been worthy of the name Athenian Hall, but the down-to-earth people of Brownington thought that the name was too showy. They preferred a simpler name, and the students started calling the building "The Stone Boarding House."

After the dormitory closed Brownington residents called it "The Old Stone Boarding House" and eventually shortened it to "The Old Stone House." Even today, when a sign bearing the words "Athenian Hall" still hangs over the front door, most people in the Northeast Kingdom call it The Old Stone House.

The Old Stone House is a plain name for an imposing structure, but the building by any name serves as a lasting memorial to the incredible physical force and spiritual power of its creator.

SCHOOL DAYS

Positioned beside the busy stagecoach route, Alexander's school prospered. Most of the students came from Orleans County, but the school drew pupils from throughout Vermont, and from as far away as Quebec and Boston. In 1841 forty-two girls and fifty-nine boys attended the Orleans County Grammar School. During the next several years, the school averaged more than one hundred students per term, and the student body was usually about 70 percent boys and 30 percent girls.

The school year was divided into four terms, and each term lasted twelve weeks. The students who attended all four terms received only four weeks of vacation time per year, about a quarter of the vacation time that school children enjoy today. Students were expected to study for ten hours a day, from 9:00 a.m. until 7:00 p.m., with only a short break for lunch. A hand bell was rung in the hallway to signal the end of each recitation period, when

This building served as the classroom building for the school in Brownington even after Alexander built Athenian Hall. It is now used as a meeting hall for the National Grange. (Author photo)

it was time to change to the next class. And each Sunday morning, every student was obliged to attend church (where Alexander resumed preaching soon after the building was completed). The students also had to attend Alexander's Bible study every Sunday evening. Evidently Alexander believed that "idle hands do the Devil's work," so he left his students little spare time to get into trouble.

More than forty students lived at Athenian Hall, where they each paid $1.50 for twelve weeks of room and board. Tuition prices for classes varied, depending on the subject. Studying vocal music cost only fifty cents per term. Languages were more expensive. "Common English" cost $2.00 per term, "higher English," Greek, Latin, Spanish, and Italian cost $3.00, and written and spoken French cost $3.50 per term. Alexander and his faculty also gave lectures in agriculture, algebra, astronomy, botany, chemistry, geology, history, philosophy, and trigonometry. Alexander was very serious about preparing his pupils for college, and his classes closely followed the courses he had taken at Middlebury College.

Although he was demanding and strict, Alexander had a good sense of humor, and he tried to make education fun for his students. He was often eager to share a laugh with his pupils. One of his favorite tricks was to give students a dose of "laughing gas." Also known as nitrous oxide, laughing gas is used as an anesthetic to reduce pain during surgery or dental work. Alexander used laughing gas for entertainment, dosing students and then encouraging them to perform strange stunts that they would have never tried unless under the influence of the gas.

Nowadays any teacher who intoxicated students with laughing gas would no doubt be arrested. But during the 1800s it was considered just a harmless prank, designed to keep the students from becoming bored. Alexander also used playful experiments with an air pump, a hand-cranked electrical generator, and other devices to produce interesting classes. And Alexander's unusual techniques certainly worked. Not only did his students learn well, they also came to respect and admire Alexander. They affectionately called Alexander "Father Twilight," or "Uncle Twilight," or sometimes "Old Twilight." He became a beloved father figure for the boys and girls under his care.

Mercy Twilight also played an important role in dormitory life. She prepared wonderful meals in the large kitchen, and the children looked up to her as a mother figure. Many of the students were far from home, and some rarely saw their real families. The academy became their "home away from home," and the Twilights and students seemed like one big family.

As in all families, though, discipline was sometimes necessary. When a boy misbehaved, Alexander subscribed to the "spare the rod, spoil the child" way of thinking shared by most parents and educators in his day. Alexander spanked unruly boys with a yard-long leather strap, often applying it with so much energy and enthusiasm that sitting down afterwards was painful for the boys, and they were certain to be on their best behavior. Sometimes a boy would try to avoid his punishment by hiding the strap, but this didn't work because Alexander kept more than one of the feared straps on hand. Alexander became well known as a strict disciplinarian, and if any boy within a hundred miles of Brownington developed a reputation as a troublemaker, he was usually sent to Alexander's school for a serious education.

Although Alexander was also stern with the girls, he didn't use the strap on them. Instead he relied on words and the threat of more severe punishments to influence their conduct. Despite his sometimes harsh disciplinary techniques, Alexander influenced his students far more through respect than intimidation. His students held Alexander in such high esteem that they were eager to win his approval and avoid his scolding. He earned their respect by being fair, and by setting a good example of how to work hard, play hard, maintain high ideals, and accomplish difficult goals.

Alexander also taught his pupils to fulfill their responsibilities, no matter how unpleasant the circumstances. For example, whenever anyone died and was buried in Brownington, one of the boys had to climb into the belfry in the wooden schoolhouse to ring the bell while the funeral procession slowly passed by the school on its way to the cemetery. During the winter months, when temperatures in northern Vermont often plunge far below zero, the freezing wind howled through the open belfry as the poor lad shivered in the wind and pulled the bell rope until the procession passed. In Alexander's school, severe conditions or unusual difficulties were not good reasons to abandon an assignment. Alexander wasn't interested in excuses; he wanted results.

Alexander achieved wonderful results with his students, and several became very successful. James and William Strong, the sons of a Brownington trustee, had especially distinguished careers. James, the elder brother, became an educator like Alexander, and he eventually served as the president of Carleton College in Minnesota. William began working for the Atchison, Topeka and Santa Fe Railroad as a telegraph operator when he was eighteen years old. He worked hard, received regular

The wooden desks used by Alexander's students are preserved in Athenian Hall. (Author photo)

promotions, and took over as president of the railroad when he was forty-four years old. Later William returned to northern Vermont in his private railroad car. He built a summer home in Brownington, and in the 1890s constructed an observatory tower on Prospect Hill near Athenian Hall.

Other prominent graduates of the school included Tyler Stewart, who served as the United States Consul to Spain; Brigadier General Stephen P. Jocelyn, who fought in the Civil War and the Spanish-American wars; H. S. Tarbell, who was superintendent of schools at Indianapolis and Providence; Henry Stron, mayor of Beloit, Wisconsin; and many other distinguished businessmen, politicians, military officers, teachers, and missionaries. These people became successful through their own efforts, of course, but it is obvious that Alexander's school gave them the skills they needed to succeed.

Alexander was a hero to his pupils. He believed that teaching young people is the most important job of all, and he strove to improve the minds and souls of his students. He used laughter, music, entertainment, and literary exhibitions to make learning fun, and he influenced their characters as well as their scholarship. It can be said that his contributions to his students' well-being were even more enduring than the granite building in which he molded their personalities.

ALEXANDER IN THE LEGISLATURE

Soon after Alexander finished building the stone dormitory in 1836, his school was threatened with a loss of funds. The town of Craftsbury chartered the second grammar school in Orleans County and asked the state legislature for some of the money that otherwise would have gone to Alexander's school. As usual when he faced a problem, Alexander chose to confront it head-on. He believed that the funding issue was too important to assign to anyone else, so he ran for the state legislature himself. Brownington citizens realized that Alexander was the best man to plead their cause, and they elected him to the Vermont House. It is likely that few knew that by voting for Alexander, they were making history—Alexander Twilight was the first African-American to serve in a state legislature in the United States.

Alexander was reluctant to leave his school, his wife, his home, and his students, but he wanted to preserve the funding. He found a Dartmouth College graduate, a man named Redfield, who was willing to serve as interim headmaster at the Brownington school while Alexander was away. Alexander bid his students farewell, kissed Mercy goodbye, and boarded the stagecoach for Montpelier.

Alexander was sworn in as a member of the Vermont House on October 13, 1836. He discovered that several of the bills voted on by the legislature were, in his opinion, a waste of time. For instance, one bill that didn't pass would have forbidden the legislative members from wearing hats at a joint assembly.

Most of the bills were not so silly, though. Many articles of unfinished business were left over from the previous legislative session, including an act to increase the bounty on wolves. Most farmers hated wolves because they killed sheep and other livestock, so the state paid people to kill them. Vermont paid a total of $320.00 for wolf certificates in 1836. Another interesting article was an "act to prevent the establishment of monasteries, nunneries, and other superstitious communities, within this state."

The article of unfinished business that really drew Alexander's attention, though, was an "act to divide the funds arising from the grammar-school lands in the county of Orleans, between grammar schools situated at Brownington and Craftsbury." Instead of being voted on right away, this bill was referred to the Committee on Education.

Alexander was appointed to serve on the five-person Committee on Education. The members of the committee were selected to study bills relating to education and then report their findings to the rest of the House. Serving on the committee was a good position for Alexander, because it gave him an opportunity to influence the vote. Unfortunately, Alexander was not a good politician. He was a man of action, unaccustomed to the pleading and dealing of politics, and he had a hard time persuading legislators to change their votes.

While he was trying to influence the upcoming vote on the school funding, Alexander voted on several other bills. He voted yes on a conservation bill "to preserve the fish in Hinesburgh pond." He voted against "an act laying a tax of four cents on the town of Roxbury." He voted to pay members of the General Assembly for their mileage expenses, and he voted against "an act establishing permanent salaries for certain officers." He took these and other bills seriously, but his main concern was always the school funding.

Finally on November 14, 1836, the bill about dividing the funds from the Grammar School Lands in Orleans County was read for a deciding vote. Alexander made a motion to dismiss the bill. A total of twenty-nine legislators voted to dismiss the bill, while 137 voted not to dismiss it. Alexander argued that one good school was better than two average schools. He said that if the small funds were divided now, they might be split into smaller shares later, and soon there wouldn't be enough money for any of the schools to do well. He presented a good case, but the majority was against him, and the bill passed.

Alexander's failure to sway the vote in his favor was a bitter pill to swallow. He worried that his school might not receive enough funding to survive. But Alexander was too tough to be discouraged for long, and he continued with the political business at hand. Perhaps as revenge for his own defeat, Alexander voted against "an act in favor of Caledonia County Grammar School."

Alexander voted in favor of abolishing imprisonment for debt. From his own childhood experiences, he knew that poor people, despite their best efforts, sometimes have a hard time paying their bills. Alexander didn't believe that people should be jailed just because they didn't have enough money. The majority of the legislators disagreed with him, however, so imprisonment for debt remained legal.

Alexander voted to raise money for land surveys. He voted to incorporate the Bank of Poultney and the Bank of St. Albans. And he voted several times against referring bills to future legislative sessions, because Alexander was the kind of man who liked to get things settled instead of putting things off.

When the legislative session was completed in early 1837, Alexander knew that his political career was finished. He was not a politician at heart, and he never ran for office again. Alexander failed at his primary goal as a legislator, but he succeeded in gaining a place in history. The second African-American to serve in a state legislature was Benjamin Arnett of Ohio, who was elected fifty years later. The second African-American to serve in the Vermont legislature, an orchardist from Shoreham named William J. Anderson, was not elected until the 1940s, more than a century after Alexander served.

TRUSTEE TROUBLE

Despite Alexander's concerns about funding, his school prospered for the decade following his session as a legislator. As many as 140 children per term attended the school, which succeeded so well that Alexander was issued a new contract in 1844 and signed on to teach for two more years at a higher salary of $232.00 per year, paid quarterly.

During that happy decade, as Alexander prepared his students for the challenges of life, he became used to running the school as he saw fit. He believed that he knew what was best for his school and his students, and he sometimes resented the interference of the trustees. Some of the trustees thought that Alexander was too dominating, and their relationship became strained.

In addition to Alexander, who was a teacher as well as the principal, the school employed three or four other teachers during each term. Usually one or two of the teachers were women, but in 1846 there were no women on the faculty. The trustees asked Alexander to hire a woman teacher, probably reasoning that it was improper to operate a co-ed boarding school with an all-male faculty. Alexander agreed, but he couldn't locate a satisfactory woman teacher who would come to Brownington for the modest salary available.

The friction increased between Alexander and the trustees, and they criticized Alexander for not hiring a female teacher as they had requested. The need for a female teacher was not necessarily their main concern, though; they probably were more disturbed by the fact that Alexander hadn't obeyed them.

Next, the trustees charged that Alexander had disobeyed the school's by-laws. The by-laws were eight rules governing the Orleans County Grammar School. The rules stated when school would be in session; the type of behavior and academic requirements expected of the students; and the duties and responsibilities of the principal. The trustees accused Alexander of defying the by-law that required students to attend church on Sunday. This seems unlikely, considering Alexander's strong religious background, so the charge may have been more of a political tactic than a genuine complaint. The accusation understandably angered Alexander, and the dispute worsened.

The situation came to a head in 1847. It is unclear whether Alexander was actually fired, or if he resigned—he was probably given a choice and resigned in order to avoid being fired. Either way, at the age of fifty-two, after eighteen years at the school in Brownington, Alexander stepped down as principal.

Alexander must have been heartbroken at the thought of leaving his beloved students and Athenian Hall. He sold the dormitory to the trustees for $3,000, which was a small fortune in 1847, but the money probably seemed unimportant to Alexander compared to the loss of everything that he had achieved in Brownington. As part of the deal with the trustees, Alexander promised not to teach in Orleans County.

Alexander still intended to teach, however. He moved with Mercy to a Canadian town called Shipton, which is now known as Richmond, Quebec. Shipton was a growing town scheduled to become an important junction on a new railroad, but it had no school. It seemed like a perfect place for Alexander to open his own academy.

As he searched for a location for the school, Alexander certainly found nothing as grand as the granite building he had left behind. He settled for a humble site on the upstairs floor of the St. Francis Hotel and opened Twilight's Academy in 1847. Alexander taught school there for the next two years, although it must have been difficult to ignore the sounds of carousing coming from the tavern downstairs.

Whenever Alexander remembered the magnificence of Athenian Hall, he was disturbed by the limitations of Twilight's Academy. But what could he do? He was no longer the mighty young man who had split apart boulders to construct a towering building on a windy hilltop. Such a spectacular feat couldn't be performed twice in one lifetime.

After operating Twilight's Academy for two years, Alexander closed the school and moved thirty-five miles south to accept a teaching position at Charleston Academy in Hatley, a Canadian town located within fifteen miles of Orleans County, Vermont. Charleston Academy was a neat, wooden-clapboard building located beside an Anglican Church in a rural town. When Alexander taught there in 1849, Charleston Academy was nineteen years old with more than one hundred students and only three teachers. In addition to teaching, Alexander was required to collect tuition fees from the students. Half of the fees that Alexander collected were handed over to the school's trustees. Alexander kept the rest of the money, which was deducted from his salary.

Alexander would have preferred being in charge of his own school, but he didn't mind working at the Charleston Academy. Living conditions were pleasant for Mercy and Alexander in Hatley, and they stayed there for three years.

Meanwhile, back in Vermont, the trustees were discovering that the school in Brownington was less successful without Alexander. His replacement, Reverend William Scales, performed his duties with spirit and devotion, but the number of students and the amount of tuition money declined steadily. A new school in Derby made things worse by drawing away some of the students and some of the state funds.

The predictions that Alexander had made as a legislator eventually came true. School funding was split into ever smaller shares as many schools sprang up across Orleans County. The small, local schoolhouses suffered from inferior equipment and poorly trained teachers because the county's modest assets were spread too thin.

After several other grammar schools were opened in Orleans County, the school near Athenian Hall became known as Brownington Academy instead of the Orleans County Grammar School. Brownington Academy continued to struggle, and in 1851, six years after Alexander had left, the Academy was forced to close.

For more than a year, the Brownington trustees disagreed about what they should do to save their failing school. While they argued, Athenian Hall stood vacant. The school remained closed for three terms. Finally the trustees decided to swallow their pride and ask Alexander to come back, so they sent a delegation on a mission to Hatley in October 1852.

Alexander was thrilled to be invited to return to Brownington as headmaster and minister, and Mercy was pleased also. Hatley was nice, but it wasn't home, and the Twilights didn't require much coaxing to agree to return to Vermont.

RETURNING HOME

Returning to Brownington was one of the happiest moments of Alexander's life. To the people who welcomed him, Alexander said, "This is the home of my choice, and here with the blessing of God I will devote myself to the interests of education."

Alexander resumed teaching at Brownington Academy and preaching at the Brownington Congregational Church, which had been built in 1841 to replace the old meeting place on the second floor of the wooden schoolhouse. Alexander felt fortunate to be back in the place that he loved the best.

When Alexander and Mercy returned from Canada, they were accompanied by an Englishman named Addison, his wife, and their four children (two sons and two daughters). The Addisons were friends of the Twilights, and they came to Vermont seeking a better life. Mr. Addison ran a mercantile store in Brownington for

Alexander preached in the Brownington Congregational Church until 1853. The church still welcomes worshipers on Sundays. (Author photo)

twelve years and also served as the postmaster. The Addison children attended Brownington Academy.

Alexander's health soon declined, and he had a hard time taking care of all of his responsibilities. A year after he returned to Brownington, Alexander felt too weak to keep up his busy schedule, so he decided to resign as minister of the Congregational Church. Alexander again placed his teaching duties ahead of his preaching duties, just as he had when he built Athenian Hall.

Alexander ran the school for another two years after resigning as minister, but in 1855 he suffered a stroke. A stroke, which occurs when not enough blood reaches the brain, damages the brain, sometimes enough to cause death. Alexander didn't die immediately, but the stroke left him paralyzed and unable to continue managing the school. Cared for by Mercy, Alexander lived for another two years. He died on June 19, 1857, at the age of sixty-one and was buried beside the Congregational Church, within sight of the granite dormitory that he had built with his own hands.

LEGACY

Without Alexander's guidance, attendance at Brownington Academy again dwindled. Competition for state funds and enrollment weakened the school, exactly as Alexander had warned when he had been a legislator. Brownington Academy struggled for two years after Alexander died, then closed in 1859.

Mercy stayed in Athenian Hall and supported herself by working as the town liquor agent, an odd occupation for a minister's widow. She lived alone in the huge building until 1865, when she sold it to Mr. Addison, the Englishman who had come down from Canada with the Twilights. Mercy moved to Derby, Vermont, where she lived until she died of gastric fever on July 27, 1878. She lies buried in the Brownington Cemetery beside Alexander, in the plots closest to the imposing building where they had spent the best years of their lives.

Alexander and Mercy Twilight lie buried in Brownington Cemetery near the Old Stone House, as Athenian Hall is now called. (Author photo)

Carved into Mercy's tombstone are the words, "Wife of A. L. Twilight, Asleep in Christ." Alexander's tombstone is engraved with the words, "The gospel I so long preached, was my support in affliction, my sure hope in death."

Samuel Read Hall taught in Brownington during the 1850s and became friends with Alexander. He also served as the minister of the Congregational Church after Alexander resigned. Hall later opened the first school designed for training teachers in America, and he is believed to have been the first educator to use a blackboard and blackboard eraser in a school. The house in Brownington where he lived from 1856 until 1877, across the road from the Congregational Church, is listed as the Samuel Read Hall House in the Brownington Historic District.

The wooden schoolhouse was moved downhill about 300 yards in 1869, and Brownington Academy reopened briefly in the 1870s as a small, local school. Nowadays the building is used as the Grange Hall. The Grange provides lectures, entertainment, and educational programs for farm families. It rents the upper part of the building from the town of Brownington. Downstairs, the Ladies Aid Society of the Congregational Church serves breakfast a few times each year.

The population of Brownington continued to grow until 1870, then started to shrink as many of Alexander's former students joined thousands of New Englanders who migrated west for better farmland and economic opportunities. As railroads became increasingly important for transporting goods and produce, hill towns like Brownington declined while valley towns connected by railroads prospered. As industry became more important, larger streams that provided water power for mills gave valley towns another advantage over hill towns. Brownington's population slowly declined over the following century.

Mr. Addison decided to move to Boston, and he sold Athenian Hall to his son-in-law, George Rice. When George Rice died, his widow, Elizabeth Addison Rice, rented rooms in the big building, and people called her operation "Grammy Rice's Boarding House." Elizabeth Rice eventually returned to Canada, and the upper stories of Athenian Hall stood abandoned. Although the first floor was almost always occupied, broken windows let rain and snow inside the upstairs rooms, and animals moved in and made their homes in the once-proud building.

In 1916, after Elizabeth Rice died, a foolish administrator wanted to destroy the magnificent building and use the granite blocks for bridge abutments! Fortunately, the Orleans County Historical Society realized the historical significance of Athenian Hall, so they negotiated to buy it for the purpose of preserving the building. It is fitting that the Orleans County Historical Society saved Athenian Hall, because Alexander Twilight was one of the original members of the Society, which formed in 1853 under the name "The Orleans County Natural and Civil History Society." Samuel Read Hall was also an original member of the Society, which is the oldest organization of its type in Vermont.

The Society succeeded in buying Athenian Hall in 1918 for $500.00. Since the building had stood empty for years, it needed repairing. The walls still stood straight and plumb, but the crumbling mortar between the stones had to be replaced. Since then a new roof has been installed and seven chimney tops were restored, but the building is basically the same now as it was in Alexander's day. Even some of the students' graffiti survives. James Addison, one of the Addison children who accompanied the Twilights when they returned from Canada, carved his name and the name of his Canadian hometown into the plaster wall of an upstairs room. Many years later, when the room was painted, a small section of the wall was left untouched to preserve his graffiti.

The Orleans County Historical Society turned Athenian Hall into a museum and invited every town in Orleans County to furnish one of the rooms with historic displays. Originally there were thirty-one rooms in Athenian Hall, but a few interior walls were removed to convert four downstairs rooms into one long room. Of the twenty-seven rooms now in the building, eleven are "Town Rooms." Open to the public since 1925, the museum also contains the Orleans County Historical

Society's wonderful collection of antique tools, furniture, and artwork.

The State of Vermont Board of Historic Sites bought Prospect Hill in 1968 to preserve the hilltop against development. Rising above the Congregational Church, Prospect Hill is the highest point in Brownington at 1,360 feet. The observatory on Prospect Hill offers stunning views of Lake Memphremagog, Lake Willoughby, the Green Mountains, and Quebec. In 1976 a replica of the 1890s observatory was built atop Prospect Hill as a town bicentennial project, and it is seasonally open to the public.

Bypassed by the railroads and abandoned by many of its ambitious young citizens, Brownington did not grow while most of the United States expanded in population and development. The fact that Brownington stayed basically the same has made the village a charming example of America's past. In order to preserve the village, the Brownington Village National Historic District was formed in 1973 and includes The Old Stone House Museum, the Congregational Church, the Twilight Homestead, Prospect Hill, the Samuel Read Hall House, the Cyrus Eaton House, and several other structures.

The Brownington Village Historic District is a popular place for school classes and other groups to visit. The Old Stone House Museum is shown by guided tour and is open from May 15 through October 15. More information about the museum may be obtained from the following address:

Orleans County Historical Society
The Old Stone House Museum
RR #1, Box 500
Orleans, VT 05860

The Old Stone House Museum displays several objects that once belonged to Alexander and Mercy, including the ox yoke and the iron pry bar that Alexander used to build Athenian Hall. A poem entitled "The Old Academy," which was written by Mary Currier Smith and dedicated to the students of Alexander Twilight, is also exhibited at the Museum.

The museum is not the only memorial of Alexander Twilight. In 1969 Lyndon State College built the Alexander Twilight Theatre, a lecture hall used for assemblies, concerts, and speeches. The hall may also be divided into three smaller sections to be used as class-

Alexander's ox yoke and pry bar are displayed on a wide windowsill in the Old Stone House Museum. (Author photo)

rooms. Alexander would be proud to know that a building named after him is being used for educational purposes.

Middlebury College has also honored the memory of Alexander Twilight by creating the Twilight Program, which invites artists and scholars from diverse backgrounds to present their skills at Middlebury. The Twilight Program also offers fellowships to minority teachers.

In 1984 Middlebury College bought a run-down brick building that had been built in 1867 and originally used as the Addison County Grammar School. After spending more than a million dollars to repair the building, Middlebury College named it Alexander Twilight Hall and included it as part of their campus. Alexander Twilight Hall has five classrooms, five seminar rooms, and twelve faculty offices, and it is located near the spot where Alexander himself attended college.

In 1995, 200 years after Alexander was born, Middlebury College displayed an exhibit in their Starr Library from September through January. Arranged by archivist Bob Buckeye, the exhibition was called "Roots, Raps, Schools, and Tools: Twilight's Education and Education's Twilight." The exhibit honored Alexander for dedicating his life to teaching the children and grandchildren of the settlers who tamed the Vermont frontier. Included in the exhibit were catalogs, lecture notes, publications that described conditions at Middlebury when Alexander was a student, and library books that Alexander had read. The exhibit stressed an important lesson: teachers should believe enough in education to make it their top priority. This is a lesson that Alexander understood perfectly.

Alexander's desk contains a few pieces of his china and several of his books, including his Bible. It is on display in the Old Stone House Museum. (Author photo)

Alexander Twilight's legacy played an important role in *A Stranger in the Kingdom,* Howard Frank Mosher's renowned novel. It features a fictional character named Pliny Templeton, who is loosely based on Alexander. In the novel, Pliny Templeton was an African-American who, like Alexander, founded an academy in northeastern Vermont. Unlike Alexander, Pliny was an ex-slave who was later murdered. A movie version of A *Stranger in the Kingdom* starring Ernie Hudson, Martin Sheen, and Jean Louisa Kelly was filmed in Vermont in 1997. The movie takes place many years after Pliny Templeton's death, but his skeleton and his legend play important roles.

Alexander Twilight was an extraordinary person by any measure, so it is a little ironic that he is best remembered today for breaking racial boundaries. It is true that he was the first African-American to graduate from an American college and the first to serve in a state legislature, but racial issues seem to have had little impact on his day-to-day life.

Alexander put no limits on his own possibilities, and those around him placed no boundaries on what he could do. With hard work and determination, he improved his own situation and favorably influenced thousands of others—he lived the American ideal decades before most non-whites were able to. Looking back, Alexander's accomplishments demonstrate just how wrong and destructive racial injustice is. Who knows how many other African-Americans would have had a powerful positive effect on their communities in Alexander's day if they simply had the opportunity?

Athenian Hall, built, according to local lore, with two hands, a strong back, and an ox, is Alexander's most visible achievement. It is the thousands of students he prepared to live productive lives, though, that are by far his most valuable legacy. It is impossible to measure just how much his teaching and his love of learning helped his students, then their children and grandchildren, but

the productivity and success enjoyed by so many graduates of his school indicate that his contributions were
enormous. Alexander always put teaching first, and it
was in teaching that he enjoyed his greatest success.

CHRONOLOGY

Date	Alexander Twilight	Vermont	North America
1791		Vermont became the 14th state.	
1795	Alexander Twilight was born in Corinth, VT.		
1800			A black man named Gabriel led a slave uprising in Virginia.
1803	Alexander was indentured to a neighboring farmer.		
1814		U. S. forces defeated the British Fleet on Lake Champlain.	
1823	Alexander graduated from Middlebury College.		
1826	Alexander married Mercy Merrill.		
1827	Alexander became a licensed minister.		
1829	Alexander became principal of the Orleans County Grammar School.		
1831			Nat Turner was hanged for leading a slave revolt.
1836	Alexander completed building Athenian Hall.		
1836	Alexander was sworn in as a member of the VT House.		

CHRONOLOGY

Date	Alexander Twilight	Vermont	North America
1843			Sojourner Truth began her reform mission.
1847	Alexander and Mercy moved to Canada.		
1849			Harriet Tubman escaped from slavery and began working on the Underground Railroad.
1852	Alexander and Mercy returned to Brownington.		
1857	Alexander died on June 19.		
1859	Brownington Academy closed.		
1865			The 13th Amendment to the United States Constitution abolished slavery.
1878	Mercy died on July 27.		
1918	The Orleans County Historical Society bought Athenian Hall.		
1969		Lyndon State College builds Alexander Twilight Theatre.	
1984		Middlebury College begins renovation of Alexander Twilight Hall.	

BIBLIOGRAPHY

Ferrin, Clark E. "Rev. Alexander Twilight," *The Vermont Historical Gazetteer*, 1877.

Hemenway, Abby Maria. *The Vermont Historical Gazetteer*. Burlington, 1871.

Herrick, Mrs. Daniel K. *Timothy Hinman's Road*. Vermont Electric Coop, 1977.

Herrick, Edith. *Brownington, Vermont*. The Magazine Antiques, 1978.

Hileman, Gregor. "The Iron-Willed Black Schoolmaster and His Granite Academy," *Middlebury College Newsletter*, 1974.

Johnson, Arthur Stoddard. *Johnson, VT*. Toledo, 1992.

Meeks, Harold A. *Vermont's Land and Resources*. The New England Press, 1986.

Mosher, Howard Frank. "Alexander Twilight and One of the Last Best Places," *Vermont Life*, 1996.

Nicolosi, Vincent. "Twilight Mystery," *Yankee*, 1986.

Orleans County Historical Society. *The Old Stone House Museum*. Northlight Studio Press, 1996.

Ripley, C. Peter. *Black Abolitionist Papers*. University of North
Carolina Press, 1992

Swett, Ralph S. "Town of Brownington: Some Historical Perspec-
tives," *Newport Express*, 1974.

INDEX

Brownington Congregational
Church, 21, 48, 49, 49,
51, 54
Ladies Aid Society, 52
Brownington Village National
Historic District, 24, 54
Buckeye, Bob, 56

-C-

Cambridge, VT, 15
Census
1800, 6
1840, 5
Champlain Presbytery, 13
Charleston Academy, 45–46
Clark, Peter, 16
Committee on Education, 40–41
Concord, NH, 17
Congregationalism, 21
Corinth, VT, 3, 4, 6
Craftsbury, VT, 17, 18, 39
Cyrus Eaton House, 54

-D-

Dartmouth College, 40
Derby, VT, 16, 18, 46

-E-

Eaton, Cyrus, 24

-F-

Ferrisburgh, VT, 14
Freeman, Martin, 11

-G-

Glover, VT, 16

"Grammy Rice's Boarding
House," 52
Granite, 25–26
Greek Revival architecture, 30–
31
Greensboro, VT, 16

-H-

Hall, Samuel Read, 51, 53
Harris, Andrew, 11
Hatley, Quebec, Canada, 46, 47
Herrick, Edith, 16
Hinman, Timothy, 16
Hinman Road, 16
History of Corinth, Vermont, The, 5
Howard, Walter E., 11

-J-

Jocelyn, Brigadier General
Stephen P., 38
Johnson, VT, 15
Johnson, William, 15

-L-

Lake Memphremagog, 54
Lake Willoughby, 54
Lyndeboro, NH, 16
Lyndon State College, 55

-M-

Merrill, Dudley (father-in-law), 12
Merrill, Polly (mother-in-law), 12
Middlebury College, 9–11, 12,
35, 56
African-American
Alliance, 10
expenses, 10